Personal Branding Blueprint

Step-by-Step Guide to Building Your Brand

Ghazwan Alemara

Copyright © 2024 Ghazwan Alemara. All rights reserved.

No part of this publication may be reproduced, distributed, or transmitted in any form or by any means, including photocopying, recording, or other electronic or mechanical methods, without the prior written permission of the publisher, except in the case of brief quotations embodied in critical reviews and certain other noncommercial uses permitted by copyright law.

For permissions requests or inquiries, please contact the publisher at hello@ghazwanalemara.com

Published by ghazwanalemara.com

Contents

Contents 3
Introduction 1
Chapter 1: Understanding Personal Branding 3
    The Essence of Personal Branding 3
    The Psychology Behind Personal Branding 7
    Personal Branding in the Digital Age 12
Chapter 2: Defining Your Unique Brand Identity 17
    Self-Assessment and Reflection 17
    Crafting Your Personal Brand Statement 22
    Identifying Your Target Audience 26
Chapter 3: Building Your Personal Brand 33
    Developing a Strong Online Presence 33
    Networking and Relationship Building 38
    Showcasing Your Expertise 43
Chapter 4: Visual and Verbal Branding 48
    Creating a Visual Identity 48
    Developing Your Verbal Identity 53
    Maintaining Brand Consistency 58
Chapter 5: Enhancing Your Brand Through Content Marketing 64
    Content Creation and Curation 64
    Developing a Content Calendar 69
    Maximizing Reach and Impact 74
Chapter 6: Case Studies and Real-Life Examples 79

    Success Stories in Personal Branding............................79
    Common Mistakes and How to Avoid Them 83
    Inspiration from Diverse Industries 89
Chapter 7: Next Steps 94
    Tools and Resources for Personal Branding..................94
    Maintaining Motivation and Momentum....................102
Conclusion...107

Introduction

Imagine waking up every day with a sense of purpose and confidence, knowing exactly who you are and how to present yourself to the world. Imagine having a unique identity that sets you apart in your personal and professional life, attracting opportunities and creating lasting impressions. This is the power of personal branding, and it's what this book is all about.

This book is your comprehensive manual for understanding and mastering the art of personal branding. In today's digital age, where everyone has the chance to be seen and heard, establishing a distinct and authentic personal brand is more important than ever. Whether you're an entrepreneur, a professional, a creative, or simply someone looking to define your identity, this book provides the essential tools and insights to help you achieve your goals.

The purpose of this book is to guide you through the process of creating, developing, and maintaining a personal brand that resonates with your true self and connects deeply with your audience. You will learn how to define your unique brand identity, build a strong online presence, and consistently communicate your message across various platforms. By the end of this book, you will have a clear understanding of what makes you unique and how to leverage that uniqueness to stand out in your industry.

The topic of personal branding is significant because it goes beyond mere self-promotion. It's about authenticity, credibility, and creating a meaningful impact. In a world where everyone is vying for attention, a well-crafted personal brand can elevate your visibility, open doors to new opportunities, and position you as a thought leader in your field. With the rise of social media and digital platforms, your personal brand can reach a global audience, making it an invaluable asset in both your personal and professional life.

This book is structured to take you step-by-step through the process of building your personal brand. We start with understanding the essence of personal branding and its importance in today's digital landscape. We then move on to defining your unique brand identity through self-assessment and reflection.

You will learn how to build a strong online presence, develop a consistent visual and verbal identity, and enhance your brand through content marketing. Real-life case studies and examples will provide inspiration and insights into successful personal branding strategies. Finally, we will explore tools and resources that can help you maintain and grow your brand over time.

Chapter 1: Understanding Personal Branding

The Essence of Personal Branding

Personal branding is more than just a buzzword; it's a fundamental aspect of how we present ourselves to the world. It's the process of establishing a unique image and identity that sets you apart from others. At its core, personal branding is about authenticity and showcasing your true self in a way that resonates with your audience. Let's delve into what makes personal branding essential and how it can impact your life.

Definition and Importance

Personal branding is the deliberate and intentional effort to create and influence public perception of an individual. By positioning yourself as an authority in your industry, you can elevate your credibility and differentiate yourself from the competition. This isn't just about self-promotion; it's about sharing your story, values, and passions in a way that connects with others on a deeper level.

In today's digital age, personal branding has become more important than ever. With the rise of social media and the internet, everyone has the opportunity to build a personal brand. This democratization means that your personal brand can reach a global audience, opening doors to opportunities that were once out of reach. Whether you're an entrepreneur, a professional, or a creative, a strong personal brand can help you achieve your goals.

Evolution of Personal Branding

The concept of personal branding isn't new. Historical figures like Napoleon, who carefully crafted his image to project power and control, understood the importance of personal branding. However, the modern iteration of personal branding began to take shape in the late 20th century with the advent of mass media.

Today, personal branding has evolved with technology. The internet has amplified the reach of personal brands, making it easier for individuals to connect with a broader audience. Social media platforms like LinkedIn, Instagram, and X (Twitter) serve as powerful tools for personal branding, allowing for real-time interaction and engagement. The evolution of personal branding reflects a shift from traditional corporate branding to a more personalized, individual-centric approach.

Napoleon Bonaparte - Historical Example of Branding. Source: vrijmetselaarswinkel.nl

Differentiating Yourself

One of the most crucial aspects of personal branding is differentiation. In a world where everyone has a platform, standing out requires a clear, distinct brand that highlights what makes you unique. This uniqueness is often rooted in your personal experiences, skills, and perspectives.

To differentiate yourself, start by identifying your core values and strengths. What are you passionate about? What expertise do you bring to the table? Use these insights to craft a personal brand that is both authentic and compelling. Remember, authenticity is key. Audiences can quickly detect insincerity, so it's vital to remain true to yourself.

Storytelling is a powerful tool in personal branding. Sharing your journey, challenges, and successes can humanize your brand and create a deeper connection with your audience. Your story should highlight not just your achievements but also the lessons learned and the values that guide you.

Consistency is another critical element. Ensure that your messaging, visuals, and overall brand presence are consistent across all platforms. This coherence helps reinforce your brand identity and makes it easier for people to recognize and remember you.

Building a strong personal brand takes time and effort, but the benefits are substantial. A well-crafted personal brand can lead to increased visibility, better job opportunities, and a more engaged network. It positions you as a thought leader in your field and can open doors to new ventures and collaborations.

Personal branding is about more than just self-promotion; it's about creating a meaningful and lasting impact. By understanding the essence of personal branding, you can start building a brand that not only sets you apart but also resonates deeply with your audience. Embrace your uniqueness, share your story, and watch as your personal brand transforms your professional and personal life.

The Psychology Behind Personal Branding

Personal branding is more than just a strategic exercise; it is deeply rooted in psychology. Understanding the psychological aspects can give you a significant edge in crafting a personal brand that not only resonates but also endures. Let's delve into how the human mind perceives and reacts to personal branding.

Building Trust and Credibility

Trust is the cornerstone of any successful personal brand. People are more likely to engage with and support individuals they trust. But how do you build this trust? It starts with authenticity. Authenticity involves being genuine and transparent about who you are, your values, and your intentions. When people sense authenticity, they feel more connected and are more likely to trust you.

Consistency also plays a critical role. Being consistent in your messaging, actions, and interactions helps establish reliability. When your audience knows what to expect from you, they feel more secure in their relationship with you. Consistency doesn't mean being monotonous; it means staying true to your core values and message across different platforms and situations.

Emotional Connections

Emotions drive human behavior more than logic does. To build a strong personal brand, you need to tap into the emotional aspects of your audience. Storytelling is a powerful tool for this. Sharing your personal stories, challenges, and triumphs can create a deep emotional bond with your audience. These narratives make you relatable and human, allowing people to see parts of themselves in your journey.

Another way to forge emotional connections is through empathy. Showing genuine interest in your audience's needs, concerns, and aspirations fosters a sense of understanding and care. When people feel understood and valued, they are more likely to develop a strong emotional connection with your brand.

The Influence of First Impressions

First impressions are lasting impressions. Research shows that people form an opinion about someone within the first few seconds of meeting them. This initial perception can be challenging to change, so making a positive first impression is crucial.

Your appearance, body language, and communication style all contribute to the impression you make. Dressing appropriately, maintaining good posture, and exhibiting confident yet approachable behavior can positively influence how others perceive you. Your online presence also contributes to first impressions. A well-designed website, professional social media profiles, and high-quality content can help create a strong initial impact.

Leveraging Social Proof

Social proof is the psychological phenomenon where people look to others to determine their actions. In personal branding, social proof can take the form of testimonials, endorsements, and visible connections with other reputable individuals or brands. When others vouch for your credibility and expertise, it reinforces your brand's trustworthiness.

Showcasing positive feedback, highlighting your collaborations, and displaying your achievements can significantly boost your personal brand's perception. People are more likely to trust and engage with you when they see that others do too.

The Power of Reciprocity

Reciprocity is a powerful psychological principle where people feel obligated to return a favor when someone does something for them. In the context of personal branding, this can be leveraged by providing value to your audience without expecting immediate returns. Offering valuable content, helpful advice, or free resources can create a sense of indebtedness, encouraging your audience to support you in return.

Being generous with your knowledge and time not only helps build a loyal following but also positions you as a trusted authority in your field. Over time, this goodwill can translate into stronger relationships and greater influence.

Managing Perceptions

Perception is reality when it comes to personal branding. How people perceive you directly impacts their willingness to engage with you. It's essential to manage these perceptions carefully. This involves actively shaping your narrative and controlling the messages you send out.

Pay attention to the details that contribute to your overall image, from the words you use to the visuals you share. Regularly seeking feedback and being open to adjustments can help ensure that the way you are perceived aligns with your intended brand image.

Understanding the psychology behind personal branding gives you the tools to build a more impactful and enduring brand. By focusing on trust, emotional connections, first impressions, social proof, reciprocity, and perception management, you can create a personal brand that resonates deeply with your audience and stands the test of time. This psychological foundation, combined with strategic actions, will help you navigate the complexities of personal branding and achieve lasting success.

Personal Branding in the Digital Age

The digital age has revolutionized the way we build and manage personal brands. With the internet and social media, individuals now have unprecedented opportunities to establish their presence and connect with a global audience. Understanding how to navigate this digital landscape is crucial for effective personal branding.

Social Media Icons. Source: vecteezy.com

Impact of Social Media

Social media platforms have become essential tools for personal branding. They offer a space where you can share your expertise, insights, and personal stories with a wide audience. Platforms like LinkedIn, Instagram, X, and Facebook allow you to showcase your professional achievements, engage with your audience, and build a network.

LinkedIn is particularly valuable for professional branding. It serves as a digital resume where you can highlight your skills, experience, and endorsements. Regularly posting articles, sharing updates, and engaging with industry groups can position you as a thought leader in your field.

Instagram and X offer more casual, yet equally powerful, platforms for personal branding. Instagram's visual nature allows you to share a behind-the-scenes look at your life and work, making your brand more relatable. X is excellent for sharing quick insights, participating in trending conversations, and connecting with influencers.

Effective use of social media requires consistency and authenticity. Regularly update your profiles, share content that reflects your brand, and engage with your audience in a genuine manner. Social media is not just a broadcast tool; it's a platform for building relationships.

Online vs. Offline Branding

While the digital realm offers immense opportunities, it's important to integrate your online and offline branding efforts. Your personal brand should be cohesive and consistent across all touchpoints.

Offline, your personal brand is reflected in how you present yourself in person, whether at networking events, conferences, or in everyday interactions. Your communication style, body language, and even your attire contribute to your brand perception.

Online, your website, social media profiles, and digital content form the core of your personal brand. Your website serves as your digital headquarters, providing a comprehensive view of who you are, what you do, and how you can be contacted. Ensure it is professional, user-friendly, and up-to-date.

Consistency between your online and offline presence builds trust and credibility. When people meet you in person after interacting with your online brand, there should be a seamless transition. This consistency reinforces your brand identity and makes it memorable.

Navigating Digital Landscapes

Navigating the digital landscape requires a strategic approach. It's not enough to simply be present online; you need to actively manage your digital footprint.

Start by conducting a personal audit of your online presence. Search for your name and review what comes up. Ensure that your profiles on various platforms are up-to-date and reflect your current brand. Remove any outdated or irrelevant content that doesn't align with your brand identity.

Create a content strategy that aligns with your personal brand goals. This strategy should include the types of content you will create, the platforms you will use, and the frequency of your posts. High-quality content that provides value to your audience will help establish you as an authority in your field.

Engage with your audience by responding to comments, participating in discussions, and collaborating with other influencers. Building a community around your brand can amplify your reach and impact.

Stay updated with the latest trends and changes in the digital world. Social media algorithms, platform features, and user behaviors evolve constantly. Being adaptable and willing to experiment with new tools and strategies will keep your personal brand relevant and dynamic.

In the digital age, personal branding is a dynamic, ongoing process. By leveraging social media effectively, maintaining consistency between your online and offline presence, and strategically navigating the digital landscape, you can build a powerful personal brand that stands out and resonates with your audience.

Chapter 2: Defining Your Unique Brand Identity

Self-Assessment and Reflection

Building a personal brand starts with understanding who you are. Self-assessment and reflection are foundational steps in this process. They allow you to uncover your strengths, identify areas for growth, and align your personal brand with your true self.

Identifying Strengths and Weaknesses

One of the first steps in self-assessment is to take a deep dive into your strengths and weaknesses. This isn't just about what you're good at or what you struggle with; it's about understanding how these traits shape your professional and personal life.

Begin by listing your key strengths. Think about the skills and attributes that set you apart. Are you a natural leader? Do you have a knack for creative problem-solving? Are you particularly good at connecting with people? Reflect on feedback from colleagues, friends, and mentors. Sometimes, others see strengths in us that we might overlook.

Next, consider your weaknesses. This might feel uncomfortable, but it's crucial for growth. Identifying your weaknesses doesn't mean you should focus solely on them. Instead, recognize them so you can address them or find ways to mitigate their impact. For instance, if public speaking isn't your strong suit, you might choose to focus on enhancing your writing skills to communicate your ideas effectively.

Core Values and Beliefs

Your core values and beliefs are the guiding principles that shape your decisions and actions. They are central to your identity and play a significant role in personal branding. Understanding and articulating these values helps ensure your brand is authentic and resonates with your audience.

Take some time to reflect on what truly matters to you. What are the principles you live by? Integrity, creativity, empathy, innovation—these are examples of core values that might resonate with you. Think about how these values influence your behavior and decision-making. When your personal brand aligns with your core values, it becomes more genuine and trustworthy.

Key Elements of Brand Identity. Source: medium.facilelogin.com

Passion and Purpose

Passion and purpose are the driving forces behind a compelling personal brand. They fuel your motivation and give meaning to your work. Identifying what you are passionate about and understanding your purpose can set the direction for your personal brand.

Start by asking yourself what excites you. What are the activities or topics that you find yourself drawn to, even when you're not obligated to engage with them? Your passions are often clues to your purpose. Next, consider how these passions can be integrated into your professional life. How can you use them to add value to your work and to the lives of others?

Purpose goes beyond personal satisfaction; it's about making a difference. Reflect on how your skills and passions can contribute to a larger goal. For example, if you are passionate about education, your purpose might be to inspire and empower others through knowledge-sharing. When your personal brand is anchored in a clear purpose, it becomes a powerful tool for connection and influence.

Tools and Techniques for Self-Assessment

Several tools and techniques can aid in your self-assessment journey. Personality tests like the Myers-Briggs Type Indicator (MBTI), StrengthsFinder, or the Enneagram can provide valuable insights into your personality traits and strengths. While these tools should not define you, they can offer a framework for understanding yourself better.

Journaling is another effective method. Regularly writing down your thoughts, experiences, and reflections can help clarify your values, passions, and goals. It creates a space for honest self-exploration and helps track your progress over time.

Seeking feedback from others is equally important. Constructive criticism from trusted colleagues, mentors, or friends can provide new perspectives and highlight areas you might not see yourself. Be open to this feedback and use it to refine your understanding of your strengths and areas for improvement.

Aligning with Your True Self

Self-assessment and reflection are not one-time activities. They are ongoing processes that evolve as you grow and change. The insights you gain from these practices should inform how you present yourself to the world. Your personal brand should be a true reflection of who you are, encompassing your strengths, values, passions, and purpose.

When your personal brand aligns with your true self, it resonates more deeply with your audience. Authenticity builds trust and creates meaningful connections. By understanding and embracing your unique qualities, you can craft a personal brand that not only stands out but also feels true to who you are.

Self-assessment and reflection lay the groundwork for a strong personal brand. They help you understand your unique attributes, align with your core values, and pursue your passions with purpose. As you continue this journey of self-discovery, remember that your personal brand is a dynamic expression of your evolving self. Stay true to your journey, and let your personal brand grow with you.

Crafting Your Personal Brand Statement

Your personal brand statement is a concise declaration that encapsulates who you are, what you do, and what sets you apart. It serves as the foundation of your personal brand, guiding all your branding efforts and helping you communicate your unique value effectively. Crafting a compelling personal brand statement requires introspection, clarity, and a deep understanding of your strengths and goals.

Developing a Clear Vision

The first step in crafting your personal brand statement is to develop a clear vision of what you want to achieve. This involves reflecting on your professional journey, your personal values, and your long-term goals. Think about what drives you and where you see yourself in the future. Your vision should be aspirational yet attainable, providing a direction for your branding efforts.

Ask yourself questions like:

- What are my core values?
- What am I passionate about?
- What do I want to be known for?
- What impact do I want to make?

Answering these questions will help you clarify your vision and provide a solid foundation for your personal brand statement.

Creating a Compelling Message

With a clear vision in mind, the next step is to craft a message that communicates your unique value. Your personal brand statement should be concise, memorable, and authentic. It should clearly articulate what you do, how you do it, and why it matters.

Consider the following structure:

- **Who you are**: Start with your professional identity or role.
- **What you do**: Highlight your key skills or areas of expertise.

- **Why it matters**: Explain the impact or benefit of your work.

For example, a personal brand statement could be: "As a digital marketing strategist, I help small businesses grow their online presence through innovative and data-driven campaigns that drive measurable results."

This statement clearly defines who the person is, what they do, and the value they provide. It's specific, focused, and easy to understand.

Aligning with Your Goals

Your personal brand statement should align with your professional goals and reflect the direction you want to take your career. It should serve as a guiding star, helping you make decisions and stay focused on your objectives.

Revisit your statement periodically to ensure it still aligns with your goals and aspirations. As you grow and evolve, your personal brand statement might need adjustments to reflect your new experiences and ambitions.

Consider how your statement positions you in your industry. Does it highlight your unique selling points? Does it set you apart from your peers? Your personal brand statement should position you as a thought leader or an expert in your field, making it clear why someone should choose you over others.

Authenticity and Consistency

Authenticity is key to a compelling personal brand statement. It should reflect your true self, not a persona you think others want to see. Authenticity builds trust and credibility, which are essential components of a strong personal brand.

Consistency is equally important. Your personal brand statement should be reflected in all your branding efforts, from your online profiles to your networking interactions. This coherence helps reinforce your brand identity and makes it more memorable.

Avoid jargon or overly complex language. Your statement should be easily understood by a wide audience, including those outside your industry. Keep it simple, clear, and impactful.

Examples of Personal Brand Statements

Here are a few examples to inspire you:

1. "I am a passionate educator dedicated to inspiring lifelong learning through innovative teaching methods and personalized learning experiences."

2. "As a healthcare professional, I provide compassionate and patient-centered care that improves the quality of life for my patients."

3. "I am a creative graphic designer who transforms ideas into visually stunning designs that communicate powerful messages and captivate audiences."

Each of these statements is clear, specific, and highlights the unique value the individual brings to their field.

Crafting your personal brand statement is an ongoing process that requires reflection, clarity, and authenticity. By developing a clear vision, creating a compelling message, aligning with your goals, and ensuring authenticity and consistency, you can craft a personal brand statement that effectively communicates your unique value and sets the foundation for a strong personal brand.

Identifying Your Target Audience

Knowing your target audience is crucial for effective personal branding. Your brand will resonate more deeply when it speaks directly to the needs, interests, and aspirations of your intended audience. Identifying who you want to reach and understanding their characteristics can help tailor your message and ensure it has the desired impact.

Understanding Market Needs

The first step in identifying your target audience is understanding the broader market needs. What problems are you uniquely positioned to solve? What value can you provide that others cannot? This requires a deep dive into your industry, your competitors, and the gaps that exist within the market. Conducting market research, reading industry reports, and staying updated on trends can provide valuable insights.

Consider who would benefit most from your expertise or services. Are there specific demographics, industries, or professional groups that align with what you offer? Narrowing down your audience based on these factors will help focus your branding efforts and make your messaging more precise.

Creating Audience Personas

To gain a clearer picture of your target audience, create detailed personas. These are fictional but realistic representations of your ideal audience segments. Think about the characteristics that define them—age, gender, occupation, education, interests, and challenges. What motivates them? What are their goals?

For example, if you are a career coach, one of your personas might be a mid-career professional seeking advancement. This persona might be a 35-year-old marketing manager who wants to move into a leadership role but feels stuck. Understanding the specific needs and pain points of this persona helps you craft content and messages that speak directly to their situation.

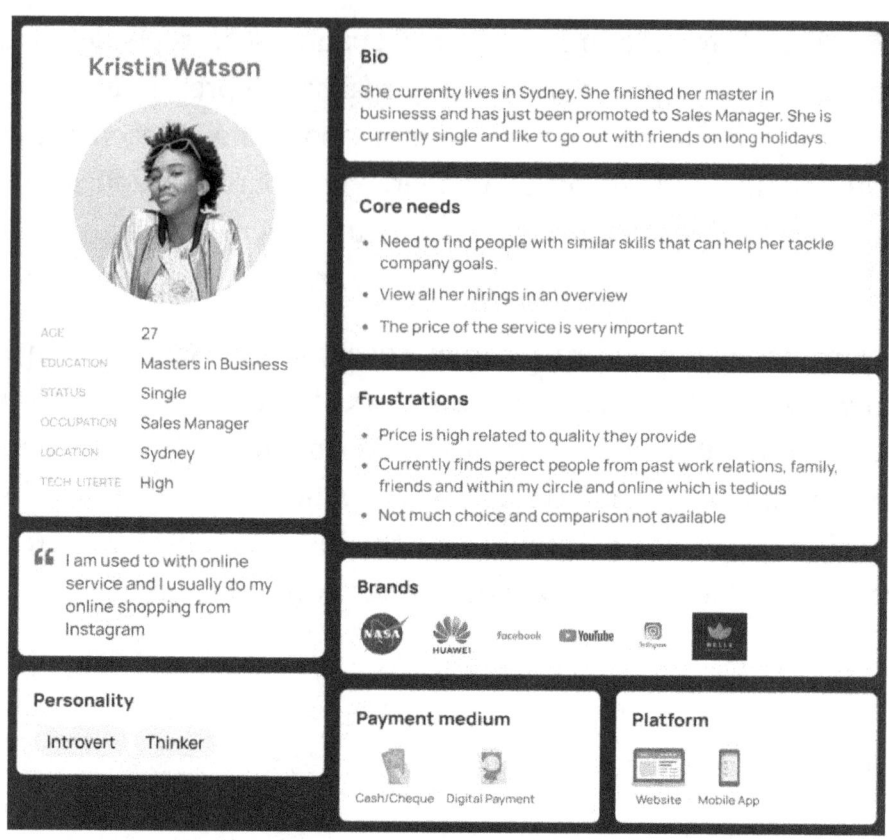

Audience Personas in Action. Source: maze.co

Engaging with Your Audience

Once you have a clear understanding of your target audience, the next step is engaging with them directly. Social media platforms, professional networks, and industry events are excellent venues for interaction. Pay attention to the discussions happening within these spaces. What questions are people asking? What topics generate the most engagement?

Participate in these conversations by providing valuable insights, answering questions, and sharing relevant content. This not only positions you as an authority but also helps you learn more about your audience's preferences and needs. Direct engagement allows you to refine your understanding and adjust your branding strategy accordingly.

Tailoring Your Message

With a deep understanding of your target audience, you can tailor your message to resonate more effectively. This involves using the language and tone that appeals to them, addressing their specific needs, and highlighting the benefits you offer.

For instance, if your target audience is young entrepreneurs, your messaging should be energetic, forward-thinking, and solution-focused. Use case studies and success stories that reflect their ambitions and challenges. If your audience consists of seasoned professionals, a more sophisticated, experience-based approach might be appropriate.

Tailoring your message also means choosing the right platforms to reach your audience. Different segments prefer different types of content and media. Younger audiences might engage more with video content on platforms like YouTube or TikTok, while professionals might prefer in-depth articles on LinkedIn or industry-specific forums.

Monitoring and Adjusting

Identifying your target audience is not a one-time task. It's an ongoing process that requires constant monitoring and adjustment. Use analytics tools to track engagement with your content, gather feedback, and measure the effectiveness of your branding efforts. Pay attention to which messages resonate and which do not.

Be open to evolving your personas and strategies based on the data you collect. The market and audience preferences can shift, and staying attuned to these changes will help keep your brand relevant and effective. Regularly revisiting and refining your understanding of your target audience ensures that your personal brand continues to grow and connect with the right people.

In summary, identifying your target audience involves understanding market needs, creating detailed personas, engaging directly with your audience, tailoring your message, and continuously monitoring and adjusting your strategy. This focused approach will help you build a personal brand that not only stands out but also deeply resonates with those you aim to reach.

Chapter 3: Building Your Personal Brand

Developing a Strong Online Presence

In today's digital world, having a strong online presence is essential for personal branding. It's not just about being visible; it's about being recognized and respected in your field. Building this presence requires strategic planning, consistent effort, and a clear understanding of your brand's message.

Creating a Professional Website

Your website is the cornerstone of your online presence. It's your digital headquarters where people can learn about you, your work, and how to connect with you. A professional website should be visually appealing, easy to navigate, and rich with relevant content.

Start by selecting a domain name that reflects your personal brand. Ideally, this should be your name or a variation of it. Choose a clean, modern design that aligns with your brand's aesthetics. The website should load quickly and be mobile-friendly, as many users will access it from their smartphones.

Include key sections like an About page, a portfolio or blog, and contact information. The About page should provide a concise but compelling overview of who you are and what you do. Use your portfolio or blog to showcase your expertise and share valuable insights. Regularly updating your content keeps your audience engaged and positions you as an active professional in your field.

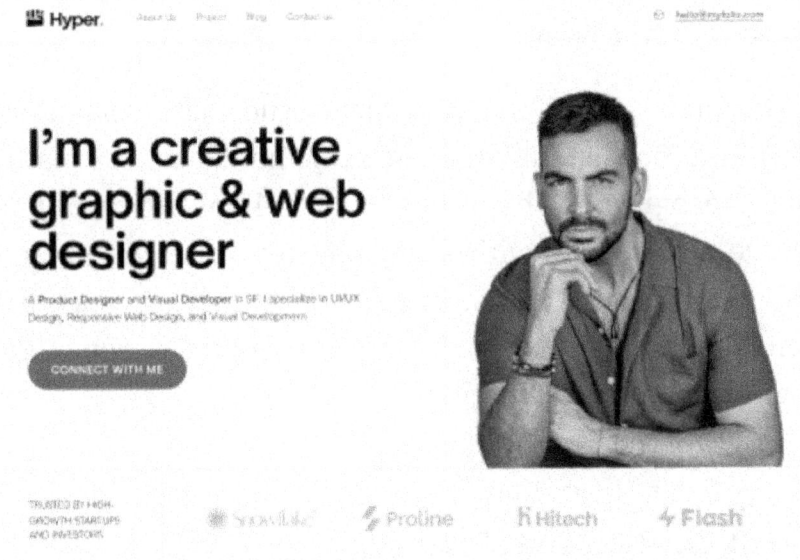

Professional Website Layout. Source: webflow.com

Optimizing Social Media Profiles

Social media platforms are powerful tools for expanding your reach and engaging with your audience. To maximize their potential, your profiles must be optimized to reflect your personal brand consistently.

Start with LinkedIn, the go-to platform for professional networking. Ensure your profile picture is high-quality and professional. Write a headline that captures your expertise and interests. Your summary should be concise, highlighting your skills, experience, and what you offer. Regularly post updates, share relevant articles, and engage with your connections to keep your profile active.

On Instagram and X, use your bio to succinctly communicate your brand. Consistently use the same handle across platforms for easy recognition. Share content that aligns with your brand's message and engage with your followers through comments, likes, and direct messages. Visual consistency, such as using a specific color palette or filter, can enhance your brand's recognition on these platforms.

Content Creation and Sharing

Creating and sharing valuable content is crucial for building a strong online presence. Content is your way of demonstrating expertise, engaging with your audience, and adding value to your community.

Identify the types of content that best suit your brand and audience. This could include blog posts, articles, videos, podcasts, or social media updates. Your content should address the interests and needs of your target audience while showcasing your knowledge and skills.

Establish a content calendar to ensure consistent posting. Consistency is key to maintaining an active online presence and keeping your audience engaged. Use SEO strategies to increase the visibility of your content. Incorporate relevant keywords, use compelling headlines, and ensure your content is easy to read and share.

Engagement is just as important as content creation. Respond to comments, participate in discussions, and connect with other influencers in your field. This interaction helps build a community around your brand and increases your visibility.

Leveraging Email Marketing

Email marketing remains one of the most effective ways to maintain direct communication with your audience. Building an email list allows you to share exclusive content, updates, and personalized messages with your followers.

Create a sign-up form on your website and offer an incentive for joining your list, such as a free e-book or access to exclusive content. Send regular newsletters that provide valuable insights, updates on your work, and opportunities for engagement. Personalize your emails to make your audience feel valued and connected to your brand.

Email marketing should be an extension of your online presence, reinforcing your brand's message and keeping your audience engaged.

Monitoring and Analyzing Your Online Presence

Regularly monitoring and analyzing your online presence is essential for understanding what works and what needs improvement. Use tools like Google Analytics to track your website traffic and user behavior. Social media platforms offer insights into engagement metrics such as likes, shares, and comments.

Pay attention to the feedback you receive from your audience. Constructive criticism can provide valuable insights into areas where you can improve. Celebrate your successes, but also be willing to adapt and change your strategy based on what the data tells you.

Developing a strong online presence is an ongoing process that requires dedication and adaptability. By creating a professional website, optimizing social media profiles, consistently creating and sharing valuable content, leveraging email marketing, and monitoring your efforts, you can build a personal brand that stands out in the digital landscape.

Networking and Relationship Building

Networking and relationship building are vital components of personal branding. These interactions expand your reach, enhance your reputation, and open doors to new opportunities. Building strong, genuine connections can significantly amplify your personal brand's impact.

The Foundations of Effective Networking

Effective networking starts with a genuine desire to connect and build relationships, not just a strategy to advance your personal brand. Authenticity is key. People can sense when interactions are purely transactional, which can undermine trust. Approach networking with a mindset of mutual benefit and shared growth.

Begin by identifying the networks and communities that align with your professional goals and interests. These could be industry-specific groups, professional associations, or even online communities. Engage actively by participating in discussions, attending events, and contributing value. The goal is to become a recognizable and respected figure within these circles.

Leveraging Professional Connections

Professional connections can provide invaluable support and resources throughout your career. Cultivating these relationships involves more than just exchanging business cards or LinkedIn invites; it requires ongoing engagement and reciprocity.

Maintain regular contact with your network through personalized messages, updates, and sharing relevant content. Show appreciation for their achievements and offer help when you can. For instance, if a connection is looking for a job, refer them to opportunities within your network. This not only strengthens your relationship but also positions you as a valuable and supportive contact.

Mentorship is another powerful aspect of leveraging professional connections. Seek mentors who can provide guidance and insights based on their experiences. At the same time, be open to mentoring others. This reciprocal relationship enriches your network and fosters a community of shared knowledge and support.

Building a Supportive Community

A strong personal brand thrives within a supportive community. Building such a community involves creating spaces where people can connect, share ideas, and support each other's growth. This can be achieved through both online and offline efforts.

Organize and participate in networking events, workshops, and seminars. These gatherings provide opportunities to meet new people, share your expertise, and learn from others. Online, consider starting a blog, podcast, or social media group focused on your area of expertise. Consistently providing valuable content and facilitating discussions will attract like-minded individuals and foster a sense of community.

Actively listen to your community's needs and feedback. This helps you stay relevant and responsive, ensuring your personal brand remains aligned with the interests and concerns of your audience. By fostering a community that feels heard and valued, you reinforce your position as a trusted and influential figure.

The Power of Strategic Alliances

Strategic alliances with other professionals and brands can significantly enhance your personal brand's visibility and credibility. Collaborations allow you to tap into new audiences, share resources, and co-create value.

Identify potential partners who share your values and goals. These could be industry leaders, complementary service providers, or influencers within your field. Approach collaborations with a mindset of mutual benefit. Propose projects or initiatives that provide value to both parties and their audiences.

Joint ventures, co-authored content, and cross-promotions are effective ways to leverage strategic alliances. These partnerships not only expand your reach but also add depth and diversity to your personal brand. The key is to choose alliances that are authentic and aligned with your brand's identity and objectives.

Nurturing Long-Term Relationships

Building a network is not a one-time effort but an ongoing process of nurturing relationships. Long-term relationships require consistent attention and genuine care. Regularly check in with your contacts, celebrate their milestones, and offer support during challenging times.

Transparency and honesty are critical in maintaining trust. Be open about your intentions and honor your commitments. When people know they can rely on you, your relationships will deepen, and your personal brand will benefit from a reputation of integrity and dependability.

Adaptability is also essential. As you and your contacts grow and evolve, your relationships should too. Stay attuned to changes in their needs and interests, and be willing to adjust how you engage and collaborate. This flexibility ensures that your relationships remain relevant and mutually beneficial over time.

Networking and relationship building are essential for creating a robust personal brand. Authenticity, ongoing engagement, and a genuine interest in mutual growth form the foundation of strong professional relationships. By leveraging connections, building supportive communities, forming strategic alliances, and nurturing long-term relationships, you can amplify your personal brand's impact and create a network that supports and enhances your professional journey.

Showcasing Your Expertise

Showcasing your expertise is a vital component of personal branding. It not only establishes your authority in your field but also builds trust and credibility with your audience. Here's how you can effectively demonstrate your skills and knowledge.

Public Speaking and Workshops

One of the most impactful ways to showcase your expertise is through public speaking and conducting workshops. These platforms allow you to share your knowledge with a live audience, creating an immediate and powerful connection.

Begin by identifying opportunities to speak at industry conferences, seminars, and local events. Volunteering to speak on panels or lead discussions can also be a great starting point. Tailor your presentations to address the needs and interests of your audience, providing valuable insights and actionable advice.

Workshops offer a more interactive setting where you can engage with participants on a deeper level. They allow you to demonstrate your expertise in a practical, hands-on manner. Designing workshops that solve specific problems or teach new skills can significantly enhance your reputation as an expert.

Writing and Publishing Content

Another effective way to establish your expertise is by writing and publishing content. This can include blog posts, articles, white papers, and books. Written content allows you to delve into topics in detail, showcasing your depth of knowledge and analytical skills.

Start a blog on your website where you regularly post articles related to your field. Share your insights, research findings, and professional experiences. Writing guest posts for reputable industry blogs and websites can further extend your reach and credibility.

Consider publishing a book if you have extensive knowledge on a subject. A well-researched and professionally written book can position you as a leading authority in your field. E-books and white papers are also valuable resources that can be offered as downloadable content on your website.

Leveraging Media and Press

Getting featured in the media is a powerful way to showcase your expertise to a wider audience. Media coverage can come in the form of interviews, guest appearances on podcasts, and features in industry magazines and newspapers.

Reach out to journalists and media outlets that cover your industry. Offer to provide expert commentary on relevant topics or contribute articles. Being quoted in articles or appearing on TV and radio shows can significantly enhance your visibility and credibility.

Podcasts are particularly effective as they allow for in-depth discussions on topics related to your expertise. Consider starting your own podcast or becoming a regular guest on existing ones. This medium provides a platform to share your insights and connect with a dedicated audience.

Building an Online Portfolio

An online portfolio is an essential tool for showcasing your expertise. It provides a centralized location where potential clients, employers, and collaborators can see your work and learn more about your skills and achievements.

Your portfolio should include samples of your work, such as articles, case studies, projects, and presentations. Include detailed descriptions of each piece, highlighting the skills and knowledge used to complete them. Testimonials from clients or colleagues can add credibility and provide social proof of your expertise.

Regularly update your portfolio to reflect your latest work and achievements. This demonstrates your ongoing commitment to your field and keeps your audience engaged.

Engaging with Your Community

Engaging with your professional community is a subtle yet powerful way to showcase your expertise. Participate in online forums, social media groups, and professional associations related to your field. Share your knowledge by answering questions, contributing to discussions, and providing support to peers.

Hosting webinars and live Q&A sessions on social media platforms can also be effective. These interactive formats allow you to demonstrate your expertise in real-time and build a rapport with your audience.

Mentorship is another avenue for showcasing your expertise. By mentoring others in your field, you not only share your knowledge but also reinforce your own understanding and skills. Mentorship positions you as a leader and a trusted source of advice and guidance.

Showcasing your expertise requires a multi-faceted approach. Through public speaking, writing, media engagement, online portfolios, and community involvement, you can effectively demonstrate your knowledge and skills. This not only enhances your personal brand but also builds a strong foundation of trust and credibility with your audience.

Chapter 4: Visual and Verbal Branding

Creating a Visual Identity

A strong visual identity is a crucial aspect of personal branding. It's the first thing people notice about your brand and can leave a lasting impression. Your visual identity encompasses everything from your logo and color scheme to your website design and social media aesthetics. Creating a cohesive and appealing visual identity helps convey your brand's personality and values effectively.

Defining Your Visual Elements

The first step in creating a visual identity is defining the core elements that will represent your brand. Start with your logo. Your logo is the cornerstone of your visual identity, so it should be memorable and reflective of your brand's essence. Consider hiring a professional designer to create a logo that is unique and versatile.

Next, choose a color scheme that aligns with your brand's personality. Colors evoke emotions and can significantly impact how your brand is perceived. For example, blue often conveys trust and professionalism, while yellow can evoke feelings of optimism and creativity. Select a primary color along with a few complementary colors to create a harmonious palette.

Typography is another critical element. The fonts you choose should be easy to read and consistent with your brand's tone. For instance, a tech brand might opt for modern, sans-serif fonts, while a creative consultancy might use more playful, handwritten fonts. Consistency in typography across all platforms enhances brand recognition.

Personal Logos Example. Source: reallygooddesigns.com

Designing Your Online Presence

Your website is often the hub of your online presence, making its design crucial. A well-designed website not only looks professional but also provides a seamless user experience. Start with a clean, easy-to-navigate layout. Avoid clutter and ensure that important information is easily accessible.

Incorporate your logo, color scheme, and typography consistently throughout your website. Each page should reflect your brand's visual identity cohesively. Use high-quality images and graphics that resonate with your brand's message and aesthetic. Invest in professional photography or stock images that align with your visual style.

Don't forget mobile optimization. With the increasing number of users accessing websites on their phones, a responsive design that adapts to different screen sizes is essential. Test your website on various devices to ensure a smooth experience for all users.

Creating Consistent Social Media Aesthetics

Social media platforms are powerful tools for personal branding, and maintaining a consistent visual identity across these platforms is key. Your profile pictures, cover photos, and posts should all align with your established visual elements.

Use the same logo and color scheme on all social media profiles. This consistency helps reinforce your brand and makes it easily recognizable. Create templates for your posts that incorporate your brand's colors and fonts. This not only saves time but also ensures visual uniformity.

Pay attention to the visual content you share. High-quality images, graphics, and videos that reflect your brand's aesthetic will engage your audience and enhance your brand's perception.

Platforms like Instagram and Pinterest, which are highly visual, particularly benefit from a well-thought-out visual strategy.

Visual Storytelling

Visual storytelling is a powerful way to connect with your audience on an emotional level. Use visuals to tell your brand's story, showcase your journey, and highlight your values. This can include everything from behind-the-scenes photos and infographics to videos and branded illustrations.

For example, share images or videos of your work process, events, or client success stories. Infographics can be an excellent way to present data or share valuable insights in a visually appealing manner. Visual storytelling helps humanize your brand and makes it more relatable.

Remember, authenticity is crucial in visual storytelling. Your audience should feel that the visuals you share are a true reflection of your brand's identity. This builds trust and strengthens the connection with your audience.

Maintaining Brand Consistency

Consistency is key in maintaining a strong visual identity. Every piece of visual content you create should align with your brand's established elements. This includes not only your website and social media but also your business cards, presentations, and any other materials that represent your brand.

Create brand guidelines that outline your visual identity elements and how they should be used. This can include specifications for logo usage, color codes, font styles, and image guidelines. Having a reference document ensures that anyone creating content for your brand adheres to the same standards, maintaining a cohesive look and feel.

A strong visual identity is essential for personal branding. By defining your visual elements, designing a professional online presence, creating consistent social media aesthetics, leveraging visual storytelling, and maintaining brand consistency, you can build a visually compelling and recognizable brand that resonates with your audience.

Developing Your Verbal Identity

Your verbal identity is a crucial aspect of your personal brand. It encompasses the words you use, the tone you convey, and the overall personality that comes through in your communication. A strong verbal identity helps you connect with your audience, build trust, and establish your unique voice in a crowded marketplace.

Crafting Your Brand Voice

Crafting your brand voice begins with understanding your core values and the message you want to convey. Your voice should reflect who you are and what you stand for. Whether you aim to be seen as authoritative, friendly, innovative, or compassionate, your brand voice should consistently communicate these qualities.

Start by identifying the adjectives that best describe your brand. Are you professional, approachable, or maybe even a bit quirky? Once you have a clear sense of these traits, use them as a guideline for all your communications. Your emails, social media posts, and even casual conversations should all reflect this voice.

Authenticity is key. Your audience will quickly sense if your voice feels forced or inconsistent. Stay true to your natural way of speaking, but refine it to align with your brand's identity. This authenticity will make your communication more relatable and trustworthy.

Effective Communication Techniques

Once you've defined your brand voice, it's time to apply it through effective communication techniques. The way you structure your messages and interact with your audience can significantly impact how your brand is perceived.

Clarity is crucial. Avoid jargon and overly complex language that might confuse your audience. Aim for simplicity and precision in your communication. This makes your message more accessible and easier to understand.

Engagement is another important factor. Use a conversational tone to make your audience feel included. Ask questions, invite feedback, and encourage interaction. This not only makes your communication more engaging but also fosters a sense of community around your brand.

Storytelling is a powerful tool in your verbal identity arsenal. Sharing personal anecdotes, case studies, and narratives helps illustrate your points and make your communication more compelling. Stories resonate on an emotional level, making your message memorable and impactful.

Consistency Across Platforms

Consistency in your verbal identity across all platforms is essential for building a cohesive brand. Whether you're writing a blog post, recording a podcast, or speaking at an event, your voice should remain consistent.

Start by creating a style guide that outlines your brand voice and communication principles. This guide should include examples of preferred language, tone, and phrasing. It serves as a reference for you and anyone else who might communicate on behalf of your brand.

When engaging on social media, tailor your voice to fit the platform while maintaining your core identity. For instance, your LinkedIn posts might be more professional, while your Instagram captions could be more relaxed and personable. Despite these adjustments, the underlying voice should remain recognizable.

Emails and newsletters are another area where consistency is crucial. Develop a template that reflects your brand's voice, and use it for all your communications. This not only ensures a consistent tone but also reinforces your brand identity every time your audience interacts with your content.

Adapting to Your Audience

While consistency is important, it's also essential to adapt your verbal identity to different segments of your audience. Different groups may respond better to different tones and styles of communication.

Segment your audience based on factors such as demographics, interests, and behavior. Tailor your messages to resonate with each segment while maintaining the core elements of your brand voice. For example, a younger audience might appreciate a more casual and playful tone, while a professional audience might prefer a more formal and authoritative approach.

Listening to your audience is crucial. Pay attention to their feedback, comments, and engagement. This will provide valuable insights into what resonates with them and allow you to refine your communication strategies accordingly.

Continuous Improvement

Developing your verbal identity is an ongoing process. As your brand evolves, so should your communication style. Regularly review your verbal identity to ensure it still aligns with your brand values and resonates with your audience.

Seek feedback from trusted colleagues, mentors, and your audience. Constructive criticism can provide fresh perspectives and highlight areas for improvement. Stay open to change and be willing to adapt your voice as needed.

Staying updated with industry trends and communication best practices is also important. The digital landscape is constantly evolving, and your verbal identity should evolve with it. Embrace new tools, platforms, and techniques to keep your communication fresh and relevant.

Developing a strong verbal identity is about more than just choosing the right words. It's about creating a consistent, authentic voice that resonates with your audience and reinforces your personal brand. By crafting a clear brand voice, using effective communication techniques, maintaining consistency, adapting to your audience, and continuously improving, you can develop a verbal identity that truly stands out.

Maintaining Brand Consistency

Brand consistency is the glue that holds all the elements of your personal brand together. It ensures that every interaction, whether online or offline, communicates the same message and reinforces your brand identity. Consistency builds trust, recognition, and loyalty among your audience, making it an essential aspect of successful branding.

Establishing Brand Guidelines

To maintain consistency, start by creating comprehensive brand guidelines. These guidelines should detail your visual and verbal identity, including logo usage, color schemes, typography, and tone of voice. Think of them as a rulebook that governs how your brand is presented across all platforms and materials.

Your logo guidelines should specify acceptable variations, minimum sizes, and spacing requirements. This ensures that your logo is always used correctly and looks professional in every context. Color schemes should include exact color codes for both print and digital media to prevent any discrepancies.

Typography guidelines should outline which fonts are used for different types of content, such as headings, body text, and captions. This creates a cohesive look and feel in all your communications. Additionally, include examples of your brand's tone of voice to ensure that the language used in your messaging remains consistent and reflects your brand's personality.

Consistent Visual Elements

Consistency in visual elements goes beyond just the logo, colors, and fonts. It includes all the imagery, graphics, and design elements associated with your brand. Ensure that all visual content, from website graphics to social media posts, adheres to your established guidelines.

Use a consistent style for photos and illustrations. If your brand uses professional, high-quality images, avoid mixing in low-resolution or amateurish visuals. If you use a specific style of illustration, stick with it to maintain a unified aesthetic.

Templates can be incredibly helpful in maintaining visual consistency. Create templates for presentations, social media posts, newsletters, and other recurring content. These templates should incorporate your brand's visual elements and ensure that each piece of content looks and feels like it belongs to your brand.

Uniform Messaging

Just as important as visual consistency is uniformity in messaging. Your audience should receive a consistent message regardless of the platform or medium. This includes the language you use, the values you communicate, and the overall tone of your content.

Develop key messages that encapsulate your brand's core values and mission. These messages should be integrated into all your communications, from website copy and social media posts to email newsletters and speeches. Consistent messaging reinforces your brand's identity and helps build a clear and recognizable voice.

Regularly review and update your content to ensure it aligns with your brand guidelines. This includes auditing your website, social media profiles, marketing materials, and any other touchpoints. Consistency doesn't mean your content needs to be repetitive, but it should always be aligned with your brand's identity and objectives.

Training and Collaboration

If you work with a team, training them on your brand guidelines is crucial. Everyone involved in creating content for your brand should understand and adhere to these guidelines. Conduct workshops or create training materials that explain the importance of brand consistency and how to implement the guidelines.

Collaboration tools can also help maintain consistency. Shared assets, like brand guideline documents, templates, and style guides, should be easily accessible to everyone on your team. This ensures that all team members are on the same page and can produce content that aligns with your brand's standards.

Monitoring and Adapting

Maintaining brand consistency is an ongoing process. Regularly monitor your brand's presence across different platforms to ensure adherence to your guidelines. Tools like social media management software and website analytics can help track how your brand is being represented and perceived.

Be open to feedback and willing to adapt. As your brand grows and the market evolves, you might need to update your brand guidelines. This doesn't mean changing your core identity but refining how you present it to stay relevant and effective.

Brand audits can be a valuable tool for maintaining consistency. Periodically review all aspects of your brand to identify any discrepancies or areas for improvement. This helps keep your brand aligned and ensures that every touchpoint reinforces your identity.

In essence, brand consistency is about creating a unified and recognizable identity that your audience can trust and rely on. By establishing clear guidelines, ensuring uniformity in visual and verbal elements, training your team, and regularly monitoring your brand's presence, you can maintain a consistent and compelling personal brand. This consistency not only builds trust and recognition but also strengthens the overall impact of your brand in the long run.

Chapter 5: Enhancing Your Brand Through Content Marketing

Content Creation and Curation

Creating and curating content is at the heart of personal branding. High-quality, relevant content can establish your expertise, engage your audience, and amplify your message. The process involves both generating original content and curating existing content that aligns with your brand.

Crafting Original Content

Creating original content allows you to share your unique perspective and expertise. Start by identifying the topics that resonate with your audience and align with your brand's mission. These could be areas where you have deep knowledge or emerging trends that interest your audience.

Writing blog posts, producing videos, and recording podcasts are all effective ways to share your insights. When crafting content, focus on providing value. Whether it's solving a problem, sharing new information, or offering inspiration, your content should always aim to benefit your audience.

Storytelling is a powerful tool in content creation. Share personal anecdotes, case studies, and real-life examples to make your content more engaging and relatable. Stories help to humanize your brand and create a deeper connection with your audience.

Utilizing Visual Content

Visual content is highly effective in capturing attention and conveying messages quickly. Incorporate images, infographics, and videos into your content strategy to make your posts more engaging. Visuals can simplify complex information and make it more digestible for your audience.

When creating visual content, maintain consistency with your brand's visual identity. Use your brand's color scheme, typography, and style guidelines to ensure that your visuals align with your overall branding. High-quality visuals not only enhance your content but also reinforce your brand's professionalism.

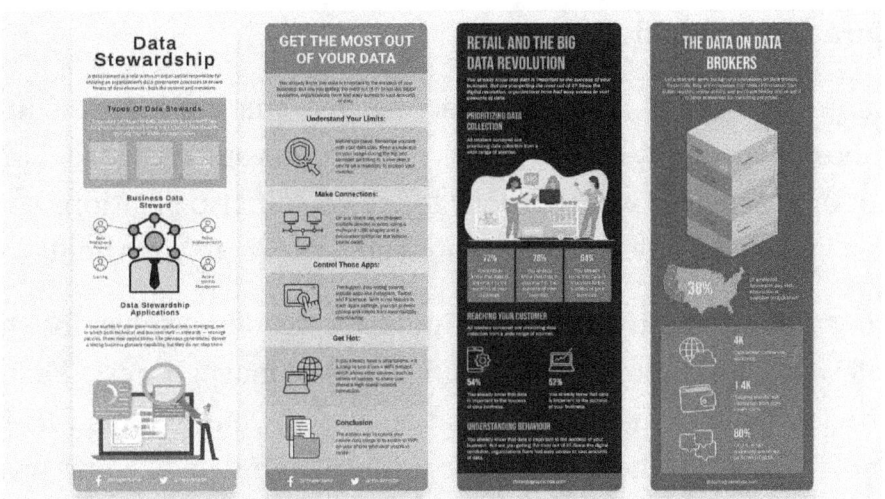

Infographic Example. Source: slidenest.com

Engaging Through Social Media

Social media platforms are essential for distributing your content and engaging with your audience. Tailor your content to fit the style and format of each platform. For example, Instagram is ideal for visual content, while LinkedIn is better suited for professional articles and insights.

Regularly posting and engaging with your audience is key. Respond to comments, participate in discussions, and share relevant updates. Social media is a two-way street, so active engagement is crucial for building a loyal following.

Curating Valuable Content

Curating content involves selecting and sharing high-quality content created by others that is relevant to your audience. This not only provides value to your followers but also positions you as a knowledgeable and well-connected expert in your field.

To curate effectively, follow industry leaders, subscribe to relevant newsletters, and join professional groups. Share articles, videos, and insights that align with your brand's values and interests. When sharing curated content, add your own commentary or insights to personalize the post and highlight its relevance to your audience.

Balancing Creation and Curation

Striking a balance between creating and curating content ensures that your audience receives a steady stream of valuable information. While original content showcases your expertise and creativity, curated content broadens your perspective and provides additional value.

Plan a content calendar that includes a mix of both. This approach not only keeps your content strategy diverse and engaging but also reduces the pressure to constantly produce new material.

Leveraging User-Generated Content

User-generated content (UGC) can be a powerful addition to your content strategy. Encourage your audience to share their own experiences and insights related to your brand. This could be through testimonials, reviews, or social media posts.

Sharing UGC not only adds variety to your content but also builds a sense of community and trust. When your audience sees real people engaging with your brand, it enhances your credibility and fosters stronger connections.

Measuring Content Performance

To ensure your content strategy is effective, regularly measure its performance. Use analytics tools to track engagement metrics such as likes, shares, comments, and views. Pay attention to which types of content resonate most with your audience.

Analyzing this data helps you refine your content strategy. Focus on creating more of what works and adjust or discard what doesn't. Continuous improvement is key to maintaining a successful content strategy.

Content creation and curation are vital for building and maintaining a strong personal brand. By producing high-quality original content, curating valuable information, and engaging actively with your audience, you can establish yourself as a trusted authority in your field. Balancing these efforts ensures a dynamic and engaging presence that keeps your audience coming back for more.

Developing a Content Calendar

Creating a content calendar is a strategic approach to planning and organizing your content. It ensures consistency, helps manage your time effectively, and allows you to align your content with your brand's goals and audience's needs.

The Benefits of a Content Calendar

A content calendar provides numerous advantages. It helps you maintain a regular posting schedule, which is crucial for keeping your audience engaged. It also allows you to plan ahead, reducing last-minute stress and giving you more time to create high-quality content. Moreover, a content calendar enables you to see the big picture, ensuring a balanced mix of content types and topics.

Setting Up Your Content Calendar

To start, choose a format that works best for you. This could be a digital tool like Google Calendar, Trello, or a simple spreadsheet. The key is to use a format that you find easy to manage and update.

Begin by identifying key dates and events relevant to your brand. These could include industry events, holidays, product launches, or significant milestones. Incorporating these dates into your calendar ensures that your content remains timely and relevant.

Next, outline the types of content you plan to create. This could include blog posts, social media updates, videos, newsletters, and more. Assign specific topics to each piece of content, ensuring a diverse range of themes that will appeal to your audience.

Planning Content Themes and Topics

To keep your content engaging and varied, plan themes for each month or week. These themes can be based on industry trends, audience interests, or your brand's goals. For example, if you run a fitness brand, you might dedicate January to "New Year's

Resolutions" and focus on workout plans, healthy eating, and motivation tips.

Once you have your themes, brainstorm specific topics under each theme. Make sure these topics align with your audience's interests and needs. Use tools like Google Trends, BuzzSumo, or keyword research to identify popular and relevant topics.

Scheduling Content

With your themes and topics in place, it's time to schedule your content. Determine the frequency of your posts based on your resources and audience engagement. For instance, you might decide to publish a blog post once a week, post on social media daily, and send out a monthly newsletter.

Enter these posts into your content calendar, specifying the type of content, the topic, and the publication date. Include deadlines for each stage of content creation, such as drafting, editing, and final approval. This helps ensure that each piece is ready to go live on schedule.

Balancing Content Types

A well-rounded content calendar includes a variety of content types. This not only keeps your audience engaged but also allows you to leverage different formats to convey your message. For example, you might mix informative blog posts with engaging videos, interactive social media posts, and in-depth white papers.

Ensure that your content calendar reflects this diversity. Plan a mix of long-form and short-form content, visual and written pieces, and interactive elements. This approach helps cater to different audience preferences and keeps your content fresh and engaging.

Reviewing and Adjusting Your Calendar

A content calendar should be a dynamic tool that evolves with your brand and audience. Regularly review your calendar to assess what's working and what's not. Use analytics to track the performance of your content, looking at metrics like engagement, reach, and conversions.

Based on these insights, adjust your content strategy as needed. If certain types of content or topics perform particularly well, consider increasing their frequency. Conversely, if something isn't resonating with your audience, re-evaluate its place in your calendar.

Stay flexible and open to change. The digital landscape is constantly evolving, and your content calendar should be able to adapt to new trends and opportunities.

Tools and Tips for Effective Management

To manage your content calendar effectively, consider using digital tools that offer collaboration features, reminders, and analytics integration. Tools like Trello and Asana can help you track tasks and deadlines, while platforms like Hootsuite and Buffer allow you to schedule and manage social media posts.

Set aside regular time to update and review your content calendar. This could be a weekly or monthly check-in where you assess your progress, make adjustments, and plan upcoming content.

Developing a content calendar is an essential step in executing a successful content strategy. It helps you stay organized, maintain consistency, and ensure that your content aligns with your brand's goals and resonates with your audience. By planning themes, scheduling content, balancing types, and regularly reviewing your calendar, you can create a powerful and effective content strategy that drives your personal brand forward.

Maximizing Reach and Impact

Creating great content is only part of the journey. To truly make a difference, you need to maximize the reach and impact of your content. This involves strategic distribution, leveraging SEO, engaging with your audience, and measuring success.

Strategic Content Distribution

To maximize reach, it's crucial to distribute your content strategically. This means sharing your content across various platforms where your audience is most active. Each platform has its own strengths and audience demographics, so tailor your content to fit each one.

For example, LinkedIn is ideal for professional insights and articles, while Instagram is great for visual content like infographics and short videos. X can be used for real-time updates and engaging in industry conversations, while YouTube is perfect for longer video content. Understanding the unique dynamics of each platform allows you to optimize your content for maximum engagement.

Additionally, repurpose your content to suit different formats and platforms. A blog post can be turned into a series of social media posts, a podcast episode, or an infographic. This not only saves time but also helps you reach a broader audience.

Leveraging SEO and Keywords

Search Engine Optimization (SEO) is essential for increasing the visibility of your content. By optimizing your content for search engines, you can attract more organic traffic and reach a wider audience.

Start by conducting keyword research to identify the terms and phrases your target audience is searching for. Tools like Google Keyword Planner or Ahrefs can help you find relevant keywords with high search volume and low competition. Incorporate these keywords naturally into your content, including titles, headings, and throughout the body.

In addition to keywords, focus on creating high-quality content that provides value and answers your audience's questions. Search engines prioritize content that is informative, well-structured, and engaging. Optimize your images with alt text, use internal and external links, and ensure your website is mobile-friendly to improve your SEO performance.

Engaging with Your Audience

Engagement is key to maximizing the impact of your content. Actively interacting with your audience not only increases visibility but also builds a loyal community around your brand.

Respond to comments and messages promptly. Show appreciation for positive feedback and address any concerns or questions. This demonstrates that you value your audience and are committed to building a genuine connection.

Encourage discussions by asking questions and inviting your audience to share their thoughts and experiences. User-generated content, such as testimonials and social media mentions, can also enhance engagement. Share and highlight these contributions to show that you value your community's input.

Collaborating with Influencers and Partners

Collaborating with influencers and partners can significantly extend your reach. Influencers already have established audiences that trust their recommendations. Partnering with them can introduce your brand to new followers who are likely to be interested in your content.

Choose influencers whose values and audience align with your brand. This ensures that the collaboration feels authentic and resonates with their followers. Joint ventures, co-authored content, and guest appearances are effective ways to collaborate and leverage each other's audiences.

Partnerships with other brands or industry leaders can also enhance your credibility and reach. Cross-promotions, joint webinars, and collaborative projects allow you to tap into each other's networks and create mutually beneficial opportunities.

Measuring and Analyzing Performance

To ensure your efforts are paying off, regularly measure and analyze your content's performance. Use analytics tools to track key metrics such as reach, engagement, conversions, and audience growth. Understanding these metrics helps you identify what's working and what needs improvement.

Set clear goals for your content strategy and regularly review your progress. For instance, if your goal is to increase website traffic, track metrics like page views, bounce rate, and average session duration. If engagement is your focus, monitor likes, comments, shares, and overall interaction rates.

Use the insights gained from analytics to refine your strategy. Experiment with different types of content, posting times, and engagement tactics to see what resonates best with your audience. Continuous improvement based on data-driven decisions will help you maximize the reach and impact of your content.

Maximizing the reach and impact of your content involves a multifaceted approach. Strategic distribution, leveraging SEO, active audience engagement, collaborations, and performance analysis all play crucial roles. By implementing these strategies, you can ensure that your content not only reaches a wider audience but also makes a lasting impact.

Chapter 6: Case Studies and Real-Life Examples

Success Stories in Personal Branding

Learning from the success stories of others can provide valuable insights and inspiration for your own personal branding journey. Here, we explore several individuals who have effectively built and leveraged their personal brands to achieve remarkable success.

Gary Vaynerchuk: The Power of Authenticity

Gary Vaynerchuk, also known as Gary Vee, is a prime example of how authenticity can drive personal branding success. Starting with his family's wine business, Vaynerchuk transformed a local liquor store into a multi-million dollar enterprise through the use of online content and social media.

Gary's unfiltered, energetic style quickly resonated with audiences. His daily videos and frequent social media posts offer practical business advice, motivational content, and a glimpse into his personal life. By being unapologetically himself, Gary built a loyal following who appreciate his honesty and insights.

His brand emphasizes the importance of hard work, self-awareness, and authenticity. Vaynerchuk's success story illustrates that staying true to yourself and consistently providing value can significantly amplify your personal brand.

Marie Forleo: Building a Community

Marie Forleo is another standout in the realm of personal branding. She started as a life coach, but her brand quickly expanded to encompass a wide range of entrepreneurial and personal development topics. Her show, MarieTV, along with her book and courses, has created a global following.

Forleo's brand is built around positivity, empowerment, and actionable advice. Her engaging and down-to-earth approach makes complex ideas accessible and relatable. Marie's ability to build a strong, supportive community has been a key factor in her success.

Her story highlights the importance of creating content that resonates deeply with your audience and fosters a sense of belonging. By focusing on community building, Forleo has established a network of loyal followers who actively engage with and promote her brand.

Neil Patel: Expertise and Consistency

Neil Patel is a digital marketing expert who has successfully built his brand by consistently sharing his knowledge and insights. Patel's journey began with his blog, where he shared detailed, actionable advice on SEO, content marketing, and online business growth.

Through relentless content creation and a deep understanding of his audience's needs, Patel established himself as a trusted authority in the digital marketing space. His consistent output of high-quality content, including blog posts, podcasts, and videos, has helped him build a vast and engaged following.

Patel's success underscores the power of expertise and consistency in personal branding. By continually providing valuable content and staying at the forefront of his field, he has built a strong, credible brand that attracts clients and followers alike.

Brené Brown: Vulnerability and Research

Brené Brown, a research professor turned public speaker and author, has made a significant impact with her personal brand centered on vulnerability, courage, and empathy. Brown's research on these topics resonated widely, particularly her TED Talk, "The Power of Vulnerability," which has millions of views.

Brown's brand is a testament to the power of combining academic rigor with personal storytelling. Her ability to present research in a relatable and engaging manner has made her a beloved figure in both academic and mainstream circles.

Her success story demonstrates that blending professional expertise with personal experiences can create a compelling and impactful personal brand. Brown's approach shows that vulnerability and authenticity can be powerful tools in connecting with and inspiring an audience.

Tim Ferriss: Experimentation and Lifestyle Design

Tim Ferriss, author of "The 4-Hour Workweek," has built his brand around lifestyle design and productivity. Ferriss's personal brand emphasizes experimentation, optimization, and unconventional approaches to work and life.

Ferriss's success can be attributed to his willingness to share his own experiments and learnings, as well as his ability to distill complex ideas into practical advice. His podcast, books, and blog have cultivated a dedicated following interested in maximizing efficiency and living an unconventional life.

Ferriss's story highlights the importance of curiosity and sharing personal experiences. By positioning himself as a guinea pig for various lifestyle experiments, he has created a unique and influential brand that continues to inspire millions.

These success stories illustrate various paths to building a powerful personal brand. Whether through authenticity, community building, expertise, vulnerability, or experimentation, these individuals have shown that a clear vision, consistent effort, and a genuine connection with your audience are key to creating a lasting and impactful personal brand. Their journeys offer valuable lessons and inspiration for anyone looking to establish or enhance their own brand.

Common Mistakes and How to Avoid Them

Building and maintaining a personal brand is a complex process that involves many moving parts. While there are numerous strategies for success, there are also common mistakes that can derail your efforts. Recognizing and avoiding these pitfalls can help you create a strong, authentic, and effective personal brand.

Overlooking the Importance of Consistency

Consistency is crucial in personal branding. It helps to establish your identity and makes it easier for your audience to recognize and remember you. One common mistake is being inconsistent in your messaging, visuals, or posting schedule. This can confuse your audience and weaken your brand.

To avoid this, develop a clear brand guideline that outlines your voice, tone, and visual elements. Stick to a regular posting schedule and ensure that your content is aligned with your brand values and goals.

Ignoring Audience Feedback

Your audience's feedback is a valuable resource for refining your brand. Ignoring their comments, suggestions, and critiques can lead to a disconnect between you and your followers. Engaging with your audience and considering their feedback shows that you value their opinions and are committed to improving.

Actively seek out feedback through surveys, polls, and direct interactions. Use this information to make informed adjustments to your content and strategy, ensuring that your brand remains relevant and responsive.

Spreading Yourself Too Thin

Trying to maintain a presence on too many platforms can dilute your efforts and lead to burnout. It's important to focus on the platforms that are most relevant to your audience and where you can consistently deliver high-quality content.

Identify the platforms where your target audience is most active and concentrate your efforts there. This will allow you to create more impactful content and engage more effectively with your followers.

Neglecting Professional Development

Personal branding isn't just about how you present yourself; it's also about what you bring to the table. Neglecting your professional development can lead to stagnation and reduce the value you offer to your audience.

Invest in continuous learning and skill development. Attend workshops, pursue certifications, and stay updated with industry trends. Sharing your learning journey and new insights can also enhance your brand's credibility and authority.

Being Too Self-Promotional

While it's important to highlight your achievements and skills, being overly self-promotional can turn your audience off. A personal brand that constantly boasts without offering value can come across as narcissistic and insincere.

Balance self-promotion with providing valuable content that addresses your audience's needs and interests. Share insights, tips, and resources that can help them. This approach builds trust and positions you as a valuable resource rather than just a self-promoter.

Failing to Adapt

The digital landscape and market conditions are constantly evolving. Failing to adapt to these changes can make your brand seem outdated and irrelevant. It's crucial to stay flexible and open to new ideas and approaches.

Regularly review your brand strategy and make adjustments based on current trends, feedback, and performance metrics. Embrace new technologies and platforms that can enhance your brand's reach and impact.

Overcomplicating Your Message

A clear and straightforward message is essential for effective communication. Overcomplicating your message with jargon, complex ideas, or unnecessary details can confuse your audience and dilute your brand's impact.

Keep your messaging simple and focused. Clearly articulate who you are, what you do, and what value you provide. This clarity helps your audience understand and connect with your brand more easily.

Ignoring Analytics

Analytics provide critical insights into how your brand is performing. Ignoring these metrics means missing out on valuable information that can help you improve your strategy and achieve better results.

Use analytics tools to track key performance indicators such as engagement, reach, and conversion rates. Regularly review these metrics to understand what's working and what needs adjustment. Data-driven decisions will help you optimize your efforts and maximize your impact.

Failing to Build Relationships

Personal branding isn't just about promoting yourself; it's also about building relationships with your audience, peers, and influencers. Failing to nurture these relationships can limit your brand's growth and influence.

Engage with your audience by responding to comments, participating in discussions, and showing appreciation for their support. Network with industry peers and collaborate with influencers to expand your reach and credibility.

Lacking Authenticity

Authenticity is the foundation of a strong personal brand. Trying to be someone you're not or presenting a false image can lead to distrust and a weakened brand.

Stay true to yourself and your values. Share your real experiences, including your successes and challenges. Authenticity resonates with audiences and builds genuine connections.

Avoiding these common mistakes requires awareness, effort, and a willingness to adapt. By staying consistent, engaging with your audience, focusing on continuous improvement, and maintaining authenticity, you can build and sustain a powerful personal brand that stands the test of time.

Inspiration from Diverse Industries

Personal branding is not confined to any single industry. Professionals from various fields have successfully built their brands by leveraging their unique skills, passions, and insights. Exploring these diverse industries can provide fresh perspectives and innovative ideas for your own branding efforts.

Fashion: The Power of Visual Storytelling

In the fashion industry, personal branding often revolves around visual storytelling. Take Chiara Ferragni, for example. Starting as a fashion blogger, Ferragni has transformed her brand into a global empire. Her success lies in her ability to curate visually stunning content that tells a story, resonates with her audience, and showcases her unique style.

Fashion professionals use imagery to create an emotional connection with their audience. High-quality photos, behind-the-scenes videos, and well-curated social media feeds are essential tools. This approach highlights the importance of aesthetics and consistent visual identity in personal branding, which can be applied across various fields.

Technology: Thought Leadership and Innovation

In the tech industry, establishing oneself as a thought leader can significantly enhance a personal brand. Elon Musk is a prime example. Musk's brand is built on his vision for the future and his relentless pursuit of innovation. He shares his insights on technology, sustainability, and space exploration, positioning himself as a forward-thinking leader.

Tech professionals can emulate this by sharing their expertise through blogs, speaking engagements, and social media. Providing valuable content, such as tutorials, white papers, and industry analyses, can help establish credibility and influence within the tech community.

Culinary Arts: Authenticity and Passion

In the culinary world, authenticity and passion are key components of personal branding. Chef Jamie Oliver's brand revolves around his genuine love for cooking and his mission to promote healthy eating. His approachable style and dedication to making cooking accessible to everyone have endeared him to a global audience.

Culinary professionals can build their brands by sharing their culinary journey, recipes, and cooking tips. Engaging with their audience through cooking demonstrations, interactive Q&A sessions, and personal stories can create a strong, authentic connection that resonates deeply with food enthusiasts.

Sports: Discipline and Motivation

Athletes often build their personal brands around discipline, motivation, and perseverance. Serena Williams, one of the greatest tennis players of all time, uses her brand to inspire others. Her story of overcoming challenges and her advocacy for equality and empowerment resonate with a wide audience.

Sports professionals can highlight their training routines, share motivational content, and engage with fans through social media and public appearances. By showcasing their dedication and achievements, they can inspire others and build a strong, motivational brand.

Entertainment: Versatility and Engagement

In the entertainment industry, versatility and audience engagement are crucial. Dwayne "The Rock" Johnson has successfully transitioned from wrestling to acting, all while maintaining a strong personal brand. His engaging personality, transparency about his journey, and connection with fans have made him a beloved figure.

Entertainers can build their brands by diversifying their skills and engaging with their audience across multiple platforms. Sharing behind-the-scenes content, personal milestones, and interactive posts can help create a dynamic and relatable brand that keeps fans engaged.

Healthcare: Expertise and Empathy

In the healthcare industry, combining expertise with empathy can create a powerful personal brand. Dr. Sanjay Gupta, a renowned neurosurgeon and medical correspondent, has built his brand on providing reliable health information and compassionate care. His ability to explain complex medical topics in an accessible way has earned him widespread trust.

Healthcare professionals can establish their brands by sharing their knowledge through articles, videos, and public speaking. Demonstrating empathy and a genuine concern for patient well-being can help build a brand that is both respected and trusted.

These examples from diverse industries illustrate that successful personal branding is about leveraging your unique qualities and connecting with your audience on a meaningful level. Whether through visual storytelling, thought leadership, authenticity, motivation, versatility, or empathy, the principles of personal branding can be adapted to fit any profession. By drawing inspiration from these varied fields, you can find innovative ways to craft and enhance your own personal brand.

Chapter 7: Next Steps

Tools and Resources for Personal Branding

Building a strong personal brand requires leveraging the right tools and resources. These can help you create, manage, and amplify your brand effectively. From design to social media management, the right tools can make a significant difference in how you present and promote yourself.

Design and Visual Content Creation

Visual content is a powerful aspect of personal branding. Tools like Canva and Adobe Spark allow you to create stunning graphics, presentations, and social media posts with ease. These platforms offer templates and drag-and-drop features, making it simple for anyone to produce professional-quality visuals.

Free LinkedIn Banner Maker on Canva. Source: canva.com

- **Canva**: User-friendly design tool with templates for social media posts, presentations, and more.

- **Adobe Spark**: Easy-to-use platform for creating graphics, web pages, and video stories.

- **Adobe Creative Cloud**: Includes Photoshop, Illustrator, and Premiere Pro for advanced design and video editing.

- **Lightroom**: Photo editing tool to enhance and manage your images.

- **Final Cut Pro**: Video editing software for creating high-quality videos.

Website Building and Blogging

A personal website serves as the hub of your online presence. Platforms like WordPress, Wix, and Squarespace offer user-friendly solutions for building a professional website without requiring extensive coding knowledge. These platforms provide customizable templates that can be tailored to reflect your brand's identity.

- **WordPress**: Powerful platform for building websites and blogs with extensive customization options.
- **Wix**: Drag-and-drop website builder with a variety of templates and features.
- **Squarespace**: Elegant website builder known for its design-oriented templates.
- **Medium**: Blogging platform to share your insights and reach a broader audience.

Social Media Management

Managing multiple social media accounts can be overwhelming. Tools like Hootsuite, Buffer, and Sprout Social streamline this process by allowing you to schedule posts, track engagement, and manage all your accounts from one dashboard. These tools provide analytics to measure the performance of your posts, helping you refine your social media strategy.

- **Hootsuite**: Schedule posts, manage multiple social media accounts, and track analytics.

- **Buffer**: Plan, schedule, and analyze social media content with ease.

- **Sprout Social**: Comprehensive social media management tool with robust analytics and reporting features.

- **Later**: Visual content calendar for planning and scheduling Instagram posts.

Email Marketing

Email marketing remains a highly effective way to reach and engage with your audience. Platforms like Mailchimp, Constant Contact, and ConvertKit offer tools for building email lists, designing newsletters, and automating email campaigns. These tools provide templates and drag-and-drop editors to create visually appealing emails that align with your brand.

- **Mailchimp**: Popular email marketing platform with automation and analytics features.

- **Constant Contact**: Easy-to-use tool for creating email campaigns and managing email lists.

- **ConvertKit**: Email marketing tool designed for creators, with powerful automation capabilities.

- **Substack**: Platform for sending newsletters and building a subscription base.

SEO and Analytics

Optimizing your online presence for search engines is critical for increasing your visibility. Tools like Google Analytics and Google Search Console provide insights into your website's performance, helping you understand your audience's behavior and preferences. These tools offer data on traffic sources, user demographics, and popular content, enabling you to tailor your strategies accordingly.

- **Google Analytics**: Comprehensive tool for tracking website traffic and user behavior.

- **Google Search Console**: Helps monitor and maintain your site's presence in Google search results.

- **Ahrefs**: SEO toolset for keyword research, competitor analysis, and backlink tracking.

- **SEMrush**: All-in-one marketing toolkit for SEO, PPC, and content marketing.

- **Moz**: SEO software for improving search engine visibility and tracking keyword rankings.

Professional Development and Networking

Continuous learning and networking are key to maintaining a strong personal brand. Platforms like LinkedIn Learning and Coursera offer a wide range of courses on personal branding, digital marketing, and other relevant topics. These courses help you stay updated with the latest trends and skills.

- **LinkedIn Learning**: Online learning platform with courses on a variety of professional topics.

- **Coursera**: Offers courses from top universities and companies on many subjects.

- **Udemy**: Platform with a vast selection of courses, including personal development and marketing.

- **Meetup**: Helps you find and create local events to meet people with similar interests.

Content Management Systems

Managing your content effectively is crucial for consistency and organization. Tools like Trello and Asana help you plan, schedule, and track your content creation process. These project management tools enable you to collaborate with team members, set deadlines, and ensure that your content strategy runs smoothly.

- **Trello**: Visual project management tool for organizing tasks and collaborating with teams.

- **Asana**: Task management tool that helps teams organize and manage their work.

- **Evernote**: Note-taking app for organizing ideas, research, and content.

- **Notion**: All-in-one workspace for note-taking, project management, and collaboration.

Monitoring and Reputation Management

Maintaining a positive online reputation is essential. Tools like Brand24 and Mention help you monitor online mentions of your brand, providing real-time alerts. These tools allow you to track conversations about your brand and respond to feedback promptly, ensuring that you maintain a positive image.

- **Brand24**: Social media monitoring tool to track mentions and analyze sentiment.

- **Mention**: Real-time media monitoring tool to track your brand's online presence.

- **Google Alerts**: Free tool for monitoring the web for specific keywords and brand mentions.

- **Trustpilot**: Platform for collecting and responding to customer reviews.

Using these tools and resources can greatly enhance your ability to build and manage a strong personal brand. They provide the necessary support to create high-quality content, engage effectively with your audience, and maintain a professional and consistent online presence. By leveraging these technologies, you can elevate your personal brand and achieve greater visibility and impact.

Maintaining Motivation and Momentum

Building and sustaining a personal brand is a long-term commitment that requires consistent effort and enthusiasm. Keeping your motivation and momentum high is essential for achieving your goals and continuing to grow your brand. Here are strategies to help you stay driven and maintain your progress.

Setting Milestones and Celebrating Achievements

Breaking down your long-term goals into smaller, manageable milestones can make the journey feel more achievable and less overwhelming. Each milestone reached is a step forward and should be acknowledged and celebrated. Celebrating these small victories keeps you motivated and provides a sense of accomplishment.

For example, if your goal is to grow your LinkedIn network by 1,000 connections, set smaller milestones like reaching 100, 250, and 500 connections. Each time you hit one of these targets, take a moment to celebrate. This could be as simple as sharing your progress with your network, treating yourself to something special, or taking a short break to recharge.

Staying Connected with Your Passion

Your passion is the fuel that drives your personal brand. Regularly reconnect with what inspired you to start your journey in the first place. Reflect on your core values, interests, and the impact you want to make. This reflection helps keep your passion alive and reminds you why your efforts are worthwhile.

Engage in activities that reignite your enthusiasm. Attend industry events, participate in workshops, or read about the latest trends in your field. Surround yourself with inspiring people and ideas that motivate you to keep pushing forward.

Creating a Supportive Network

Having a strong support network is crucial for maintaining motivation and momentum. Surround yourself with people who encourage and support your efforts. This network can include mentors, peers, friends, and family members who believe in your vision and provide constructive feedback.

Join professional groups or online communities related to your field. These platforms offer opportunities to share your experiences, seek advice, and gain inspiration from others who are on a similar path. Regular interaction with a supportive community can boost your morale and keep you focused on your goals.

Keeping a Positive Mindset

A positive mindset is essential for overcoming challenges and staying motivated. Focus on the progress you've made rather than the obstacles ahead. Practice gratitude by regularly acknowledging the things you're thankful for, both in your professional and personal life.

When faced with setbacks, view them as learning opportunities rather than failures. Analyze what went wrong, learn from the experience, and use that knowledge to improve your future efforts. This resilient mindset will help you stay on track and maintain your momentum.

Staying Organized and Focused

Staying organized is key to maintaining momentum. Use tools like planners, calendars, and project management software to keep track of your tasks and deadlines. Having a clear plan and schedule reduces stress and helps you stay focused on your priorities.

Set aside specific times each day or week to work on your personal brand. Consistent, dedicated time blocks ensure that branding activities remain a priority in your busy schedule. Even if it's just an hour a day, this regular effort can lead to significant progress over time.

Seeking Inspiration and Continuous Learning

Continuous learning and seeking new inspiration are vital for keeping your brand fresh and engaging. Stay curious and open to new ideas. Read books, listen to podcasts, and follow thought leaders in your industry to gain new perspectives and insights.

Experiment with new strategies and approaches. Trying something different can reignite your excitement and provide a fresh angle for your brand. Whether it's a new type of content, a different social media platform, or a novel marketing technique, innovation keeps your brand dynamic and interesting.

Reflecting on Your Journey

Regularly take time to reflect on your branding journey. Look back at where you started, the progress you've made, and the lessons you've learned along the way. This reflection helps you appreciate your growth and reinforces your commitment to your goals.

Keep a journal or a digital document where you record your thoughts, achievements, and experiences. This practice not only helps you track your journey but also provides a source of motivation when you need a reminder of how far you've come.

Maintaining motivation and momentum in your personal branding journey involves setting clear milestones, staying connected with your passion, building a supportive network, keeping a positive mindset, staying organized, seeking continuous inspiration, and reflecting on your progress. These strategies will help you stay driven and ensure that your personal brand continues to grow and thrive over time.

Conclusion

As we come to the end of the book, it's time to reflect on the journey we've taken together and the invaluable insights you've gained along the way.

Throughout this book, we have delved into the essence of personal branding, starting with understanding what personal branding truly means and why it is so critical in today's digital landscape. We explored the steps to define your unique brand identity, emphasizing the importance of self-assessment and reflection. By identifying your core values, strengths, and passions, you can craft a brand that is both authentic and compelling.

We then moved on to the practical aspects of building your personal brand. Developing a strong online presence is crucial, and we covered the essentials of creating a professional website, optimizing social media profiles, and engaging with your audience through consistent and valuable content. You learned how to leverage visual and verbal branding to create a cohesive and recognizable identity, and the importance of maintaining brand consistency across all platforms.

Content marketing emerged as a powerful tool to enhance your brand, allowing you to showcase your expertise and connect with your audience on a deeper level. We discussed the strategies for creating and curating content, developing a content calendar, and maximizing your content's reach and impact. Real-life case studies provided inspiration and practical examples of successful personal branding in action.

The core message of this book is that personal branding is not just about self-promotion but about authenticity, credibility, and creating a meaningful impact. In an era where everyone has the opportunity to be seen and heard, establishing a strong personal brand can set you apart, open doors to new opportunities, and position you as a thought leader in your field. Your personal brand is a reflection of who you are, what you stand for, and how you want to be perceived by the world.

As you move forward, remember the significance of the principles you've learned. Personal branding is a continuous process that evolves as you grow and change. It requires consistent effort, self-reflection, and a genuine connection with your audience. By staying true to yourself and your values, you can build a brand that resonates deeply with others and stands the test of time.

In closing, I encourage you to take the insights and knowledge you've gained from this book and apply them to your personal branding journey. Embrace your uniqueness, share your story, and let your personal brand shine. Remember, the most powerful brands are those that are authentic, consistent, and driven by a clear sense of purpose. Your personal brand is your story to tell—make it a story worth remembering.

Thank you for joining me on this journey. Here's to your continued success in building a personal brand that not only sets you apart but also brings you closer to the life and career you envision. Keep pushing boundaries, stay true to yourself, and watch as your personal brand transforms your professional and personal life.

Dear Reader,

I hope you found this book insightful and valuable.

Your feedback is invaluable to me. If you enjoyed this book, I would appreciate it if you could take a moment to leave a review on the reading apps and platforms.

Thank you for your support, and I wish you all the best.

Kind regards,
Ghazwan

About the Author

Ghazwan is a passionate entrepreneur and business strategist dedicated to helping individuals and organizations achieve their full potential with a deep understanding of modern businesses' challenges and opportunities.

With a Master's degree in Computer and Systems Sciences from Stockholm University, specializing in eService design, requirement engineering, and business process management, he is equipped to innovate cutting-edge solutions.

He believes in the power of collaboration and lifelong learning, and his mission is to empower people to reach their goals and positively impact the world.

www.ingramcontent.com/pod-product-compliance
Lightning Source LLC
Chambersburg PA
CBHW050315230526
45471CB00005B/2202